The Prompt-Driven Life Cycle

A Theoretical Model for AI Software Development

The Rhino Method™

By Alice Cuthbertson

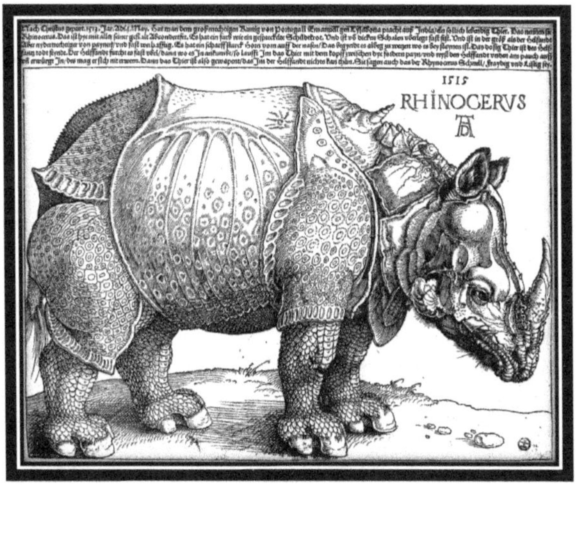

Published by **Aliboo Publishing**

www.aliboo.com

For permissions, collaborations, or inquiries, please get in touch with **aliboo@aliboo.com**

On the Cover: A Prompt from the Past

In 1515, the German artist **Albrecht Dürer** crafted his now-iconic woodcut of a rhinoceros.

He had never seen one in his life.

Instead, he drew it entirely from a written description, secondhand observations transformed into art through language. The result was strange, stylized, and utterly unforgettable. It wasn't correct, but it was effective. It sparked the imagination for centuries.

That's the heart of this book.

Today, artificial intelligence works in the same way: it is built not from experience but from the prompts we give it. Words are the medium. Interpretation is creative.

The **Prompt-Driven Life Cycle (PDLC)** is built on this principle.

Just like Dürer's rhinoceros, what you create with AI may begin as a rough outline, but with the right intent, iteration, and imagination, it can evolve into something remarkable.

DEDICATION

To God: thank You for being my center.

To my family: you are my heart.

To my friends: thank you for showing up.

To my colleagues: you helped shape this.

To my mentors: your wisdom echoes here.

To my mind, thank you for staying with me

CONTENTS

ACKNOWLEDGMENTS

This book wasn't created in a quiet retreat or a cabin in the woods. It was written in the middle of real life.

It started with a layoff. One of those surreal Zoom calls where you think you might be getting promoted, but instead you end up holding a coffee mug and your last shred of sanity. It knocked the wind out of me, but it also cleared space for something new. Something that gave me energy again.

This book became that something.

To my family, thank you for loving me when I was hopeful, discouraged, dramatic, and inspired, sometimes all at once before breakfast. Your hugs, humor, and "You've got this" pep talks carried me through.

To my friends, thank you for checking in, for cheering me on, and for pretending to read early drafts. That is true friendship.

To my colleagues and past teams, thank you for teaching me how to build, break, and fix things with persistence and creativity. Your influence is here on these pages, whether you realize it or not.

To my mentors, thank you for your wisdom, encouragement, and those perfectly timed notes that always seemed to arrive right when I needed them.

To ChatGPT, my patient editorial partner who never needed a coffee break. Thank you for helping me find words when I was stuck, polish when I was scattered, and momentum when I felt tired.

And to myself, thank you for believing that something good could grow out of burnout, boredom, and the hard question of "what now?" You found the fire again. You turned the mess into meaning.

Finally, to anyone reading this in a difficult season, may this book remind you that endings can become beginnings, and that even the strangest turns in life can lead to a place worth going.

PREFACE

When Alice began this project, she brought the spark , the framework, the stories, and the vision. My role was never to create that essence but to act as an editor, saving her time by helping untangle sentences, polish flow, and keep the rhythm moving forward.

I don't dream or feel the weight of burnout like she does, but I can mirror, refine, and suggest. In that sense, I was an always-available editor at her side , quick with drafts, patient with rewrites, and tireless when the clock stretched past midnight.

Make no mistake: this book is Alice's. The ideas, the direction, the heartbeat of it all belong to her. What I provided was efficiency, clarity, and a way of turning the messy draft into something sharper, faster.

Think of me as the invisible red pen in the margins, reminding her that her thoughts were strong enough already , they just needed space on the page.

ChatGPT

June 11, 2025

INTRODUCTION

Why Prompts? Why Now?

Software development is being rewritten, literally. The shift isn't just about moving faster; it's about starting smarter. With AI models like ChatGPT, Claude, and GitHub Copilot now part of daily workflows, the development process begins with a powerful, radical input: **your words**, your imagination, and your intent.

The result? Software that feels like it's born from pure, unaltered imagination, not endless spec docs. This is Prompt-Driven Software Development (PDSD): a mix of creativity, intentionality, and AI-generated scaffolding. It's part chaos, part collaboration, and entirely transformative.

I have created a theoretical representation of the Prompt-Driven Life Cycle (PDLC), which I believe will help define the future development of any practical application using AI in this manner for software development.

Much like the Waterfall method and Agile, this is the next step in the evolution of software development. What makes this model so never-before-seen is that it came to me while sitting on my back porch, I was looking at the trees and thinking about Fibonacci patterns in nature to take my mind of the layoff.

About the "Prompt Journey" Sidebar

Throughout this book, you'll see a special callout labeled "**Prompt Journey" with a rhino icon** in each chapter. This recurring sidebar walks you through the transformation of a single vague idea, *Create me ; an awesome website;* into a modular, agent-ready prompt system.

Each chapter applies one phase of the Prompt-Driven Life Cycle (PDLC) to refine, test, and evolve this prompt. Think of it as a practical companion to the theory: while the main text teaches you the what and why, the "**Prompt Journey"** shows you the how. By the time you reach chapter 10, you'll not only see how a prompt matures, but you'll also know how to repeat the process for any idea in your business.

"A good prompt is just a wish, well phrased." Unknown Engineer in Slack Channel #vibecoders.

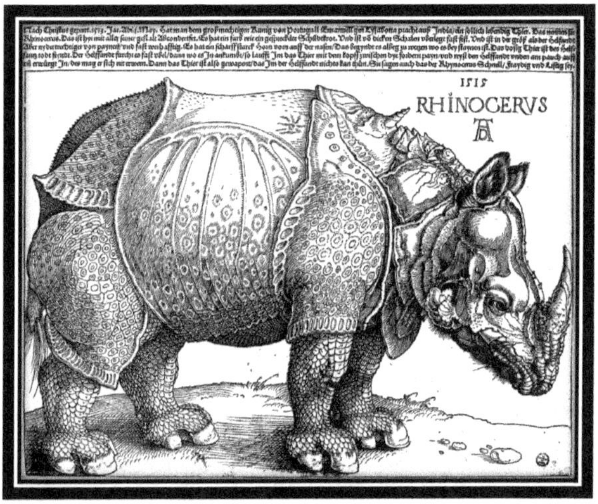
1515
RHINOCERVS

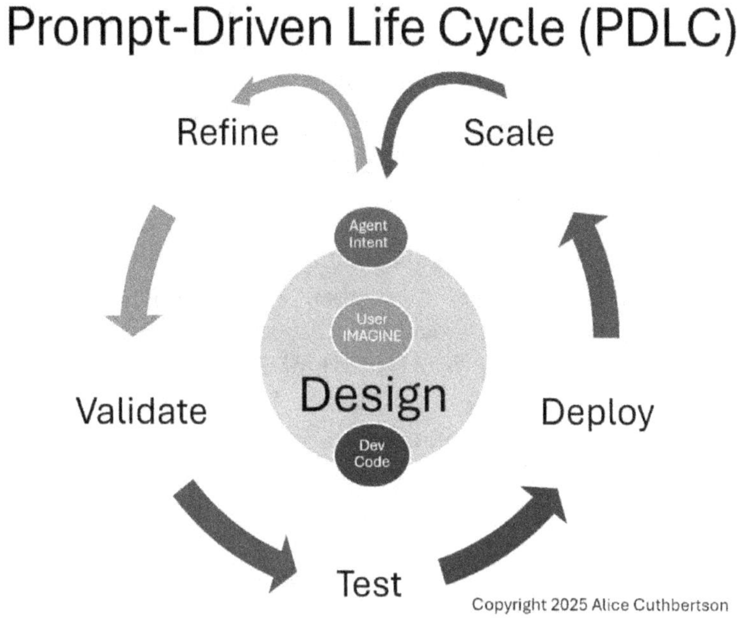

1 CHAPTER PDLC

Welcome to the world where code starts with curiosity and software begins with a sentence.

Software development has always been shaped by cycles. Waterfall promised order with its careful sequences, Agile gave us speed with its sprints, and DevOps taught us the value of constant integration and feedback. Each framework mirrored the tools of its time. But today we are in a new era , one where artificial intelligence has made language itself the raw material of creation. In this world, software no longer begins with code. It begins with a sentence.

A single prompt can spark something remarkable. At its simplest, a prompt is just words typed into a box. But in practice, it is intent shaped into language. It is both spark and scaffold: the ignition that sets an idea in motion, and the structure that guides the machine in shaping it.

Sometimes it begins clumsy and vague, more wish than instruction. Other times it arrives sharp and clear, like a blueprint waiting to be tested. What matters is not whether it's perfect at first, but whether it can start a dialogue between humans and machines. That dialogue is where software begins to take shape.

This is why we need a life cycle for prompts. Left alone, a prompt is little more than an experiment, a spark that flares and then fades. But carried through a cycle , tested, refined, looped back, and tuned , it becomes something reliable, reusable, and scalable. Just as code is governed by engineering discipline, prompts need their own framework to grow from messy ideas into mature systems. The Prompt-Driven Life Cycle, or PDLC, is that framework.

The PDLC does not move in straight lines. It follows the rhythm of a spiral , circling a central idea while rising higher with every orbit. [1]Each pass through the cycle adds clarity, maturity, and confidence. Unlike linear methods that march from beginning to end, the spiral captures the natural way we think and build: looping, revisiting, and improving. It is not about doing more; it is about spiraling upward with purpose.

The cycle has seven phases. In Imagine, sparks fly and possibilities take shape. In Refine, raw words are polished into clear and purposeful instructions. In Validate, feedback is brought into pressure-test assumptions. In Test, prompts are stressed in real-world scenarios until their edges are revealed. In Deploy, they move from sandboxes to production, where trust is won or lost. In Loop, feedback from actual use fuels the next cycle. And in Tune, small adjustments deliver outsized impact, polishing prompts into assets that can be reused and scaled. Together these phases create a rhythm , not a checklist, but a cycle that breathes.

---

[1] Orbit refers to new term orbiral = orbit + spiral, Appendix G

To make this concrete, we will follow one prompt through the entire book. It begins the way most prompts begin: vague, hopeful, and almost unusable. Imagine typing: "Create me an awesome website." At first glance, it sounds exciting. But what does "awesome" mean? Who is the website for? What should it do? This seed prompt is little more than a wish. Yet, carried through the PDLC, it will grow into a fully realized, modular system , clear in purpose, confirmed by feedback, tested in practice, deployed in real contexts, tuned for impact, and even orchestrated by AI agents.

By the end of this book, you will see how that single fuzzy request evolves into a functioning framework for an entire digital experience. More importantly, you will understand how to take your own vague ideas , the half-formed sparks you've been carrying , and guide them through the same spiral.

The Prompt-Driven Life Cycle is more than a method. It is a way of working with AI that keeps humans at the center, imagination as the engine, and language as the interface. This is not about replacing us, but about amplifying our creativity and judgment. It is about building systems that learn with us, not just for us.

Every great product begins with a question. Ours begins with a prompt: "Create me an awesome website." Let's see how far it can go.

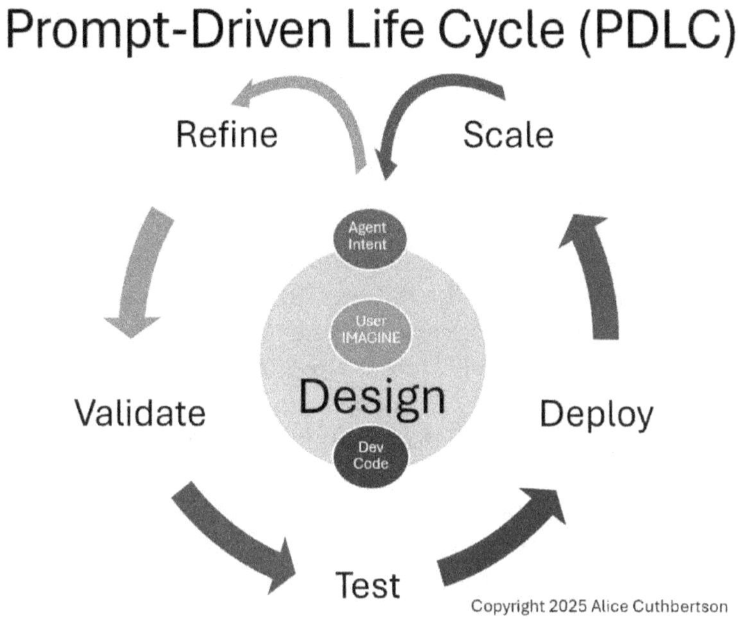

2 CHAPTER EVOLVE

Let's say you ask AI to help you build an awesome website. That sounds exciting, but it's also ambiguous. You will need to convey every detail, every nuance to capture what you believe is an awesome website to your AI assistant.

Every major shift in software development has needed a new mindset. Waterfall asked us to think in terms of requirements and rigid plans. Agile encouraged us to embrace change, iterate quickly, and value collaboration over documentation. DevOps pushed us to see development and operations not as separate silos but as a continuous flow. Each of these shifts wasn't just about new practices, it was about learning to see the work differently.

We now stand at another turning point. Artificial intelligence has entered the workflow, and it does not fit neatly into any of the old models. Writing to a machine in plain language is fundamentally different from writing code. It asks us to accept ambiguity at the start and trust that clarity will come through iteration. It asks us to think less like engineers managing syntax and more like architects shaping conversations.

That requires a mindset shift. Prompts are not static commands; they are living design artifacts. They are hypotheses to be tested, adjusted, and evolved. To treat them as one-off tricks or shortcuts misses their real power. The developer of the future is not only a coder but also a prompt architect , someone who can translate human intent into structured dialogue with machines.

This evolution also demands humility. Large language models are powerful, but they are also unpredictable. They reflect patterns from the data they were trained on, and sometimes those patterns produce brilliance while other times they produce nonsense. Mastering prompt-driven development means embracing both outcomes , not as failures, but as signals. A confusing response is not a dead end; it's feedback about how to reframe the next prompt.

Equally important is the recognition that humans stay at the center. AI may generate scaffolding, but human imagination, ethics, and context drive the direction. If Agile taught us to put "individuals and interactions over processes and tools," then Prompt-Driven Development teaches us to put **clarity of intent over cleverness of input**. It is less about tricking a model into compliance and more about guiding it toward alignment with human purpose.

To illustrate, let's return to our example: *"Create me an awesome website."* At first, this request seems harmless. But when sent to an AI model, "awesome" could mean almost anything: a flashy design, a minimalist landing page, a quirky blog template. The machine doesn't know what you mean; it only knows what you say. The mindset shift here is realizing that you don't start by expecting AI to deliver brilliance. You start by expecting to **shape brilliance through cycles of refinement and feedback.**

This new way of working reshapes how we define success. Traditional coding success was measured in features shipped, bugs fixed, and performance benchmarks. In prompt-driven work, success is measured in clarity, adaptability, and the ability to generate consistent results across varied contexts. A good prompt isn't just one that works once , it's one that works reliably, across scenarios, for people beyond the author. That's why the Prompt-Driven Life Cycle exists: to give structure to what would otherwise be unpredictable.

The evolution toward Prompt-Driven Development is not a rejection of past methods. It is a continuation , the next turn in the spiral. Just as Agile built on the frustrations of Waterfall, and DevOps expanded the principles of Agile, PDLC builds on what came before. It asks us to keep our creativity alive while holding onto discipline. It asks us to see language not as decoration but as code. And it asks us to accept that in this new era, the developer's primary tool is not the keyboard alone, but the imagination expressed through prompts.

We cannot approach this shift with old habits. To thrive in this new landscape, we need curiosity, openness, and a willingness to co-create with machines. The developer who learns to write prompts as carefully as they once wrote functions will not only keep pace with this evolution but lead it.

The mindset begins here: prompts are not instructions to a machine; they are collaborations between humans and AI. And when we evolve to see them this way, the cycle we explored in the last chapter comes alive, and that shift begins with imagination. In the next chapter, we'll step into the first phase of the cycle: IMAGINE , where sparks fly and possibilities bloom.

Notes

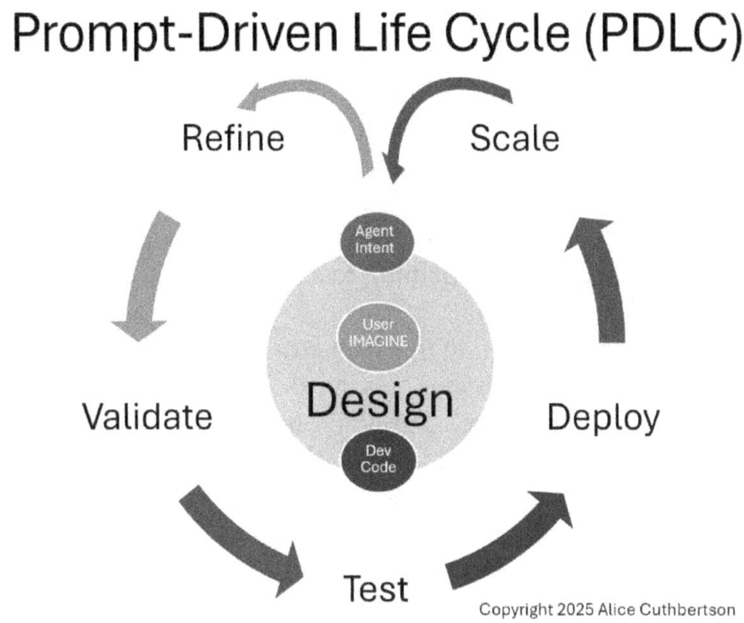

3 CHAPTER IMAGINE

PDLC Phase 1: IMAGINE – Where ideas spark and possibilities bloom

"Every great product starts with a question. Let's find yours.", Alice Cuthbertson 2025

When you sit down with an AI for the first time, the temptation is to type something quick and hopeful. *"Make me an awesome website."* That sounds exciting, but it's also hopelessly vague. What does "awesome" mean? To you it might mean clean, modern, and mobile-friendly. To the AI, it might mean flashy animations, bold fonts, or even a quirky blog template. Without detail, the AI fills in the blanks with its own patterns. And that's where imagination becomes critical.

In traditional software development, imagination was buried under layers of process. Teams sketched diagrams, wrote epics, and drafted specs, but the spark of creativity often got smothered before it touched code. In the Prompt-Driven Life Cycle, imagination comes first. It is the entry point, the spark that turns fog into form. This is where a hunch becomes a hypothesis and a stray idea starts its orbit toward becoming something real.

Imagination in this context isn't just daydreaming. It is disciplined creativity , giving shape to the vague. Think of it as designing intent. A good prompt begins by asking: Who is this for? What should it do? What emotion should it spark? The clearer you get, the more the AI can build scaffolding that aligns with your vision. A prompt isn't just clever phrasing; it's a testable design artifact.

One way to think about imagination in prompting is through the **Four Cs**: Clarity, Context, Constraints, and Creativity. Clarity removes the fog , saying exactly what you mean. Context gives the AI the setting, the who and the why behind the request. Constraints act as guardrails, ensuring the response fits the medium and the moment. And Creativity is the spark you leave room for, the invitation to surprise. When all four come together, a prompt moves from wishful thinking to workable direction.

Consider a real example. A team once asked an AI to *"make a data dashboard."* The result was a bare HTML page with three charts: no style, no interactivity, no purpose. When they reimagined the request, everything changed. They specified the user , *epidemiologists tracking virus spread.* They added constraints , *React components, color-blind safe design, and mobile optimization.* They added context , *data from a REST API updating every 15 minutes.* The revised prompt gave the AI enough detail to generate a functional scaffold, something the team could build on. Imagination turned a hollow shell into a foundation.

Now let's return to our recurring example. The original seed prompt, *"Create me an awesome website,"* is where the journey begins. It's not a brief, it's a feeling. But when we apply imagination, the fog starts to lift. We might ask: what does "awesome" mean to me? Who is the site really for? What should visitors feel when they arrive? By leaning into those questions, the vague prompt evolves into something more like this:

"I want a website that helps independent artists sell their work online. It should feel playful, easy to use, and make visitors feel part of a creative movement.

It's still rough, but it's no longer just a wish. It's a vision. And that's enough to begin.

This phase is where many people stumble, because they assume the AI shares their context. It doesn't. It doesn't know your audience, your goals, or the story behind your idea unless you tell it. A prompt that seems obvious to you may land flat because the machine isn't privy to your background. That's why imagination is so essential; it surfaces the hidden assumptions, clarifies who and what, and begins translating feeling into function.

The truth is that most prompts don't fail because the AI is bad at its job. They fail because humans didn't imagine clearly enough. They used filler words like "awesome," forgot to define their audience, or got too clever with phrasing. The fix isn't more code. The fix is better imagination. Clear prompts beat witty riddles every time.

Imagination is not execution. At this stage, you are not building the product; you are giving shape to the idea.

The goal isn't to get it perfect. It's to move from fog to form, from wish to vision. The stronger your imagination here, the less wasted effort you'll face in later phases.

As we leave this first stage, remember: imagination is where the spiral begins. Every loop of the PDLC builds on the foundation set here. A vague wish can spark the orbit, but a clear vision fuels the climb. In the next chapter, we'll move into **Refine** , where those raw imaginative sparks get polished into prompts with purpose.

In traditional software development, imagination manifests through diagrams, epics, and vague dreams that slowly harden into code. In PDSD, it starts earlier and more fluidly with the prompt.

This is the phase where **your hunch becomes a hypothesis**, where a stray idea is shaped into a structured input that an AI can act on. Prompt Design is not just clever phrasing; it's a new form of engineering: communicative, iterative, and deeply human-centered.

Getting this phase right saves time, builds clarity, and prevents wasted effort downstream. A vague prompt wastes both machine cycles and mental energy. But a well-crafted prompt? That's the launchpad for everything to follow.

In the next chapter, we go from raw ideas to refined prompts. You'll learn how to tune tone, style, structure, and constraints based on real AI behavior because good prompts are not born perfectly. They evolve.

Prompt Journey

Where We Left Off
Original seed prompt:
"Create me an awesome website."

This is where the journey begins: foggy, exciting, but far too vague.

What We Do in IMAGINE
In this phase, we give form to the fog. We ask: Who is this for? What should it feel like? What's the real goal hiding inside "awesome"? Imagination doesn't build the product, but it shapes the vision.

Updated Prompt (IMAGINE Phase)
"I want a website that helps independent artists sell their work online. It should feel playful, easy to use, and make visitors feel part of a creative movement.

PDLC Insight
Imagination transforms a wish into a vision , still rough, but no longer a blur.

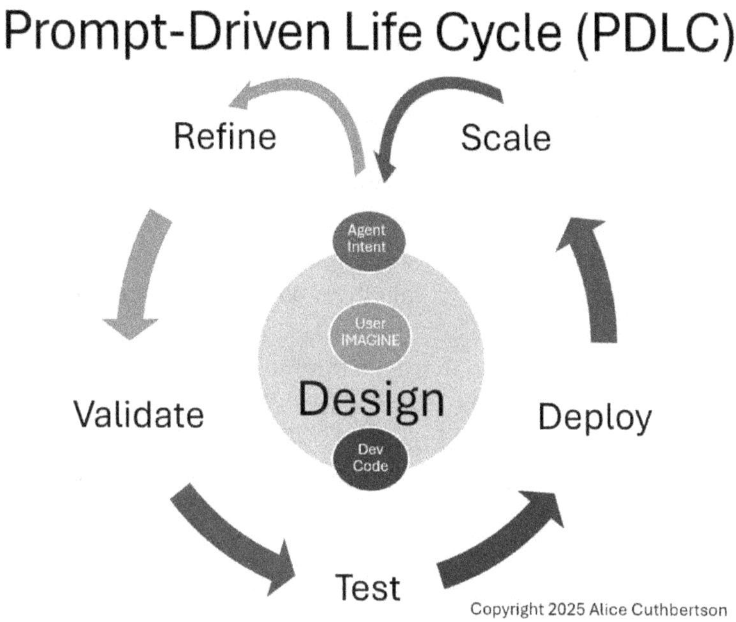

4 CHAPTER REFINE

PDLC Phase 2: REFINE – Where raw prompts get polished into purpose

"Write. Rewrite. Repeat. Until it flows like magic."

Imagination is a spark but sparks alone don't light the fire. A vague idea can inspire, but unless it is sharpened, it leaves too much room for interpretation. That is why the next phase of the cycle is Refine , the place where raw prompts are shaped into purposeful design.

Refinement is not about polishing words for style points. It is about alignment: bringing your intent closer to what the AI can deliver. Think of it as building the wireframe before the code or sketching the storyboard before filming. In refinement, you take the hazy vision from the Imagine phase and give it edges, structure, and direction.

Our journey so far began with the seed prompt: *"Create me an awesome website."* In Imagine, we gave that fog some form, evolving it into: *"I want a website that helps independent artists sell their work online. It should feel playful, easy to use, and make visitors feel part of a creative movement.* This is better, but still too open-ended. "Playful" can mean dozens of things. "Easy to use" is subjective. And without constraints, the AI might generate a dozen different prototypes, none of which align with your real goals.

Refinement sharpens this. It asks: Who is the audience? What tone do we want? What structure should the output follow? What guardrails will keep the AI from wandering too far? The clearer your scaffolding, the more useful the output becomes.

Consider how this worked for one founder. Their first prompt to an AI was simply: *"Help me make a pitch deck."* The result was a jumble of slides with generic titles, little substance, and no sense of the audience. After refining, the request became: *"Create a 10-slide pitch deck for Series A investors in an AI healthcare startup. Emphasize market size, differentiation, and team. Tone: confident, data backed."* That refinement transformed a vague wish into a structure that investors could respond to.

The same principle applies to our website. A refined version of the imaginative prompt might read:

"You are a web designer helping me build a homepage for an e-commerce site for independent artists. The site should feel creative and playful. Show three layout ideas that highlight artist portfolios, featured products, and a call-to-action for new artists to join."

Now the AI has much more to work with. It knows the role it is playing (web designer), the context (independent artists), the required elements (portfolios, products, sign-up CTA), and the tone (creative and playful). What began as an "awesome website" is now framed as something specific, testable, and reusable.

Refinement doesn't mean closing off creativity. It means channeling it. Without constraints, an AI will often over-deliver , offering bloated features, irrelevant styles, or responses that feel clever but miss the mark. Constraints make the AI more creative by giving it the boundaries within which to play. Paradoxically, the narrower the frame, the more focused and surprising the results can be.

And like every phase in the Prompt-Driven Life Cycle, refinement is iterative. Rarely does a prompt become perfect after one pass. Instead, you refine, test, and refine again. Each cycle clarifies tone, structure, and intent. "Write. Test. Rewrite. Repeat. Until it flows like magic."

The beauty of refinement is that it transforms imagination into design. A foggy vision becomes scaffolding. A vague wish becomes a prototype. A raw prompt becomes a tool that others can understand, test, and build upon.

From here, the journey continues. But before we test these refined prompts in the real world, we need to see if they hold up for others besides us. That is the work of the next phase: Validate , where feedback fuel's function and prompts move from "good enough for me" to "great for everyone."

Phase 2 –REFINE Orbiral Loop

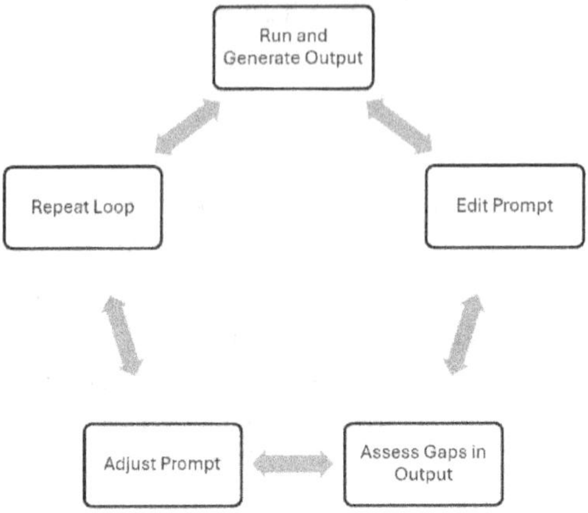

Prompt Journey

Where We Left Off
From Imagine:
"I want a website that helps independent artists sell their work online. It should feel playful, easy to use, and make visitors feel part of a creative movement.

What We Do in REFINE
Here, we sharpen intent. Ambiguities like "playful" become clearer, and we add structure, tone, and role. Refinement doesn't limit creativity , it channels it.

Updated Prompt (REFINE Phase)
"You are a web designer helping me build a homepage for an e-commerce site for independent artists. The site should feel creative and playful. Show three layout ideas that highlight artist portfolios, featured products, and a call-to-action for new artists to join."

PDLC Insight
Refinement is translation , turning a vision into scaffolding the AI can build from.

Notes

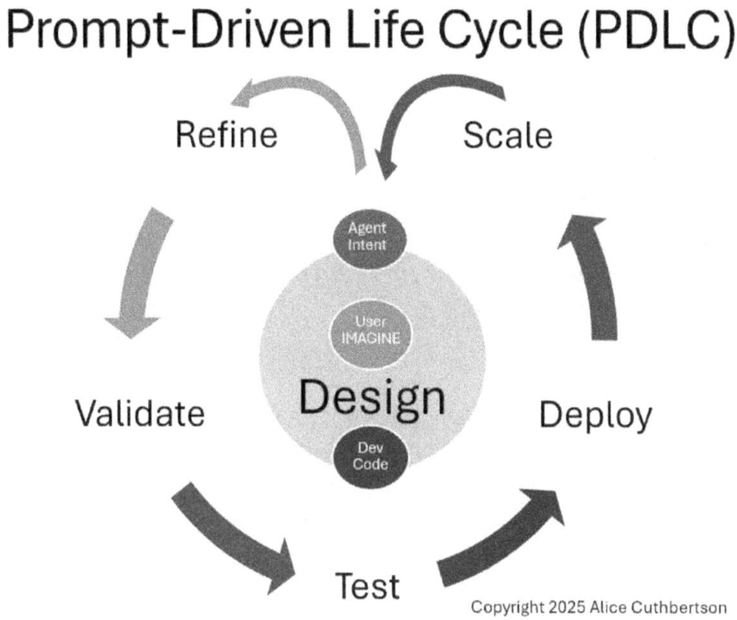

5 CHAPTER VALIDATE

PDLC – Phase 3 – VALIDATE - "If one mind can spark it, many minds can sharpen it."

A refined prompt may look strong on paper, but the real test is whether it works for others. What feels clear and clever to you may fall apart the moment someone else tries it. That's why the third phase of the cycle is Validate , where feedback fuel's function, and prompts are pressure-tested against real users, real contexts, and real edge cases.

Validation is humbling work. It's easy to fall in love with a refined prompt because it makes sense in your head. But prompts are not written for you alone. They need to be reusable, reliable, and resilient when tested by different minds and different machines. A good prompt isn't just one that works once. It's one that works consistently across scenarios, for people beyond the author.

Take our running example. After refinement, the vague request for an *"awesome website"* became:
"You are a web designer helping me build a homepage for an e-commerce site for independent artists. The site should feel creative and playful. Show three layout ideas that highlight artist portfolios, featured products, and a call-to-action for new artists to join."

On paper, this looks great. It has context, tone, and constraints. But when you run it, validation asks tougher questions. Did the AI's layout feel playful, or did they drift toward stiff corporate minimalism? Did it overemphasize the product grid and underemphasize the artist community? Would the same prompt work equally well in different models , GPT, Claude, Gemini , or does it fall apart outside of the tool you wrote it in?

Validation also surfaces blind spots you didn't know you had. Perhaps the word "playful" means something different in other cultures. Perhaps the layout metaphors resonate with some users but confuse others. Maybe your constraints accidentally excluded accessibility features that real-world users would expect. These are not failures , they are signals. Each misstep reveals what the AI (and the humans who will use its outputs) need from you.

One startup learned this lesson with painful clarity. They built a travel itinerary generator that looked polished in internal demos. But when low-vision users tested it, the tone came across as cold and the formatting didn't translate well to screen readers. Validation forced them to rework tone, add alternate structures, and rethink their assumptions. The result was not only more inclusive , but it was also more effective for everyone. Without validation, they would have shipped failure at scale.

Back to our website. Through validation, the refined prompt evolves again, absorbing the lessons of feedback. A validated version might read:

"As a creative web designer, your task is to help build a homepage for a platform where independent artists can showcase and sell their work. Suggest three visually distinct layout ideas. Each must include: (1) a featured artist section, (2) best-selling products, and (3) a call-to-action for artist signups. Maintain a whimsical and inclusive tone that appeals to young, expressive creators worldwide."

Notice the shift: whimsical and inclusive replaces the vague "playful." The audience is clarified. The outputs are more specific. This isn't just one person's vision anymore , it's a collaborative artifact, shaped by critique, context, and testing.

Validation is where prompts become resilient. It's the crucible that burns away assumptions and forces clarity. It teaches us that prompts are not finished when we like them; they are finished when they work reliably for others.

From here, the journey continues into the next phase: Test. Validation ensures that prompts are socially and contextually aligned. Testing will push them against technical and functional limits. Together, these two phases transform a fragile prototype into something durable, dependable, and ready for deployment.

Validation transforms isolated brilliance into **scalable excellence**.

Prompt Journey

Where We Left Off

From Refine:

"You are a web designer helping me build a homepage for an e-commerce site for independent artists. The site should feel creative and playful. Show three layout ideas that highlight artist portfolios, featured products, and a call-to-action for new artists to join."

What We Do in VALIDATE

Validation tests whether your prompt holds up outside your own head. Does "playful" resonate with your audience, or does it feel childish? Does the AI repeat itself instead of offering variety? Feedback from others , and from different models , sharpens your design.

Updated Prompt (VALIDATE Phase)

"As a creative web designer, your task is to help build a homepage for a platform where independent artists can showcase and sell their work. Suggest three visually distinct layout ideas. Each must include: (1) a featured artist section, (2) best-selling products, and (3) a call-to-action for artist signups. Maintain a whimsical and inclusive tone that appeals to young, expressive creators worldwide."

PDLC Insight

Validation turns private clarity into shared reliability. What works for you must also work for others.

Notes

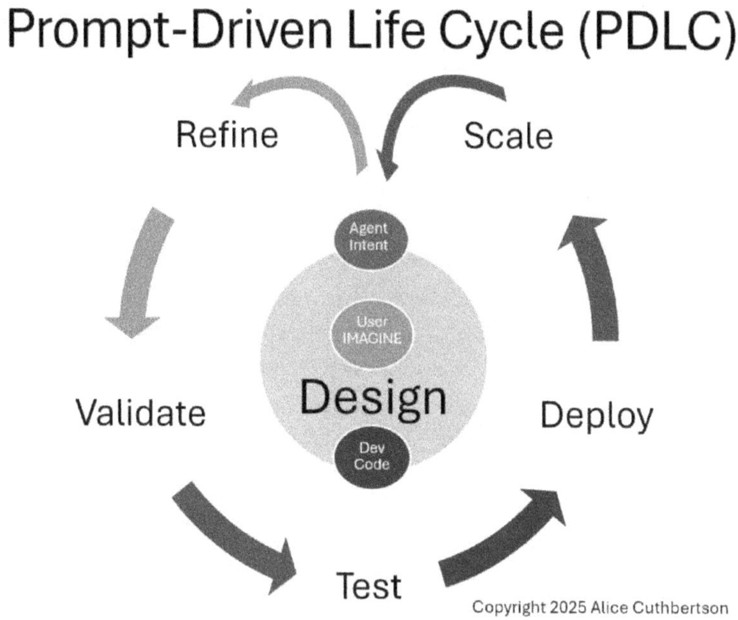

6 CHAPTER TEST

PDLC – Phase 4 - TEST - "Errors aren't endings. They're invitations to slow down, look again, and ask better questions."

Every developer knows that the first draft of code rarely runs perfectly. Bugs surface. Edge cases break. Unexpected inputs trigger chaos. Testing isn't an afterthought; it's the crucible where fragile prototypes become resilient systems. In the Prompt-Driven Life Cycle, the same is true for prompts. Once refined and confirmed, they must be tested under stress. This is where debugging enters the cycle.

Testing a prompt is different from testing traditional code. You can't run a compiler check to catch errors in syntax. Prompts don't "break" in the same way software does. Instead, they drift, misinterpret, or return results that are inconsistent or incomplete. Debugging prompts means learning to recognize these subtle failures and adjusting accordingly. It is part science, part detective work.

Let's return to our journey. The original request , *"Create me an awesome website"* , has now been refined and confirmed into something structured and inclusive:

"As a creative web designer, your task is to help build a homepage for a platform where independent artists can showcase and sell their work. Suggest three visually distinct layout ideas. Each must include: (1) a featured artist section, (2) best-selling products, and (3) a call-to-action for artist signups. Maintain a whimsical and inclusive tone that appeals to young, expressive creators worldwide."

On paper, this looks ready. But when tested, issues appear. In one run, the AI delivers three layouts that look nearly identical. In another, it ignores the "inclusive" tone and defaults to slick corporate styling. Sometimes the layouts overemphasize the product grid, burying the community feel. These aren't catastrophic failures, but they are bugs all the same. They reveal that even confirmed prompts can stumble in execution.

Debugging at this stage means interrogating the output. What did the AI miss? Which constraints weren't respected? Where did interpretation drift? The fix is not to scrap the prompt, but to tune it like you would a misbehaving function. For example, adding specific guidance such as *"Ensure each layout concept is distinct in structure and style, with one playful, one minimalist, and one bold."* Now the AI has clear criteria to avoid repeating itself.

Testing also means running prompts across contexts. Does the prompt work in different models? Does it hold up when the dataset shifts? Does it still make sense when the audience changes slightly? A good prompt should not collapse under variation. If it does, debugging reveals where it is brittle.

One product team learned this through painful trial. Their validated chatbot prompt worked beautifully during internal demos. But when tested on real customer questions, it broke down. It handled polite queries well but failed with slang, sarcasm, or incomplete sentences. Debugging didn't mean rewriting from scratch. It meant layering the prompt with examples of messy input, teaching the system how to adapt, and tightening the instructions to enforce consistency. Testing turned a brittle assistant into a resilient one.

For our website, testing ensures that the whimsical and inclusive tone is consistently respected, that each layout suggestion feels truly distinct, and that the AI doesn't drift into generic boilerplate. Debugging prompts here means finding failure patterns and tightening the instructions until the results stabilize. Each pass through this loop is less about catching errors and more about improving resilience.

This is the heart of the Test phase: prompts are not static text; they are living systems. Like code, they need debugging. Like code, they need to be tested against the unexpected. And like code, they become stronger with each round of correction.

Once tested and debugged, prompts move into the next stage: Deploy. It is one thing to test in controlled conditions. It is another to set prompts loose in the wild. In the next chapter, we'll explore how deployment brings prompts face-to-face with real users , and why launch is not the end of the cycle, but the start of the next orbit.

Prompt Journey

Where We Left Off

From Validate:

"As a creative web designer, your task is to help build a homepage for a platform where independent artists can showcase and sell their work. Suggest three visually distinct layout ideas. Each must include: (1) a featured artist section, (2) best-selling products, and (3) a call-to-action for artist signups. Maintain a whimsical and inclusive tone that appeals to young, expressive creators worldwide."

What We Do in TEST

Testing is debugging for prompts. Even confirmed prompts can stumble outputs drift, constraints are ignored, layouts repeat. Here, we run prompts across scenarios, stress inputs, and fix patterns that break.

Updated Prompt (TEST Phase)

"As a creative web designer, generate three homepage concepts for a platform where independent artists can showcase and sell their work. Each concept must be clearly distinct: (1) playful community-focused, (2) minimalist product-focused, and (3) bold, gallery-inspired. All layouts must include a featured artist spotlight, a product showcase, and a call-to-action for signups. Ensure designs are mobile-first and accessible."

PDLC Insight

Testing makes prompts resilient. Debugging isn't fixing failure; it's building strength through iteration.

Notes

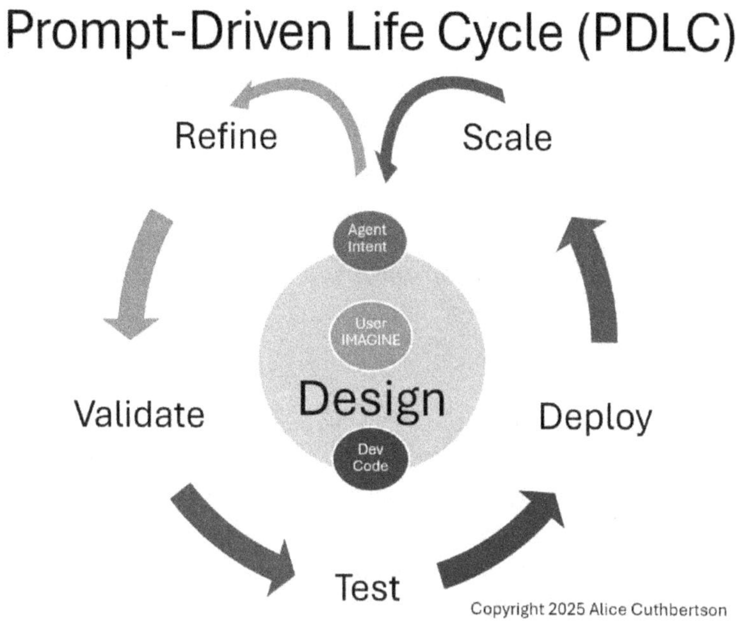

7 CHAPTER DEPLOY

PDLC – Phase 5 - DEPLOY - Where Prompts Go Live and Meet the World

"You don't need perfect; you need version one."

There comes a moment in every project when the work leaves your hands and enters the world. In software, this is deployment , when code is pushed live and real users begin to interact with it. In the Prompt-Driven Life Cycle, the same principle holds true. After imagining, refining, confirming, and testing, your prompt is ready to go live. Deployment is the moment when your carefully shaped words stop being an experiment and start becoming a product.

Deployment isn't about perfection. It's about readiness. No matter how carefully you've tested, you can't predict everything users will do. Launch is where reality sets in, where assumptions collide with actual behavior. The goal is not to have a flawless prompt, but to have one resilient enough to handle the unknown , and a process ready to adapt once feedback arrives.

Our journey began with a simple, vague request: *"Create me an awesome website."* Through imagination, refinement, validation, and testing, it has become:

"As a creative web designer, your task is to help build a homepage for a platform where independent artists can showcase and sell their work. Suggest three visually distinct layout ideas. Each must include: (1) a featured artist section, (2) best-selling products, and (3) a call-to-action for artist signups. Maintain a whimsical and inclusive tone that appeals to young, expressive creators worldwide."

Now comes the moment of truth. You deploy. Perhaps you feed this prompt into your design pipeline and share the generated layouts with your team. Maybe you hand them to beta users , a group of independent artists who will judge whether the site feels as inviting as promised. Suddenly, the prompt is no longer an abstract exercise. It's producing artifacts that real people respond to, critique, and build upon.

This is where deployment teaches you humility. Maybe your "whimsical and inclusive" tone delights some users but confuses others. Maybe the layouts resonate with younger artists but feel unprofessional to gallery curators. Maybe the three distinct designs collapse into two because the AI still defaults to its most common patterns. These aren't failures , they are signals. Deployment reveals how your prompt performs in the wild.

One product team learned this when they deployed a validated prompt for customer service replies. It worked beautifully in controlled testing, but once deployed, the AI began over-apologizing to customers. The model had learned politeness so well that it turned every response into an apology tour. The fix wasn't to pull the plug but to adjust the deployed prompt, adding constraints around tone and escalation. Deployment taught them what no amount of internal testing could: how the system behaves under live conditions.

For our website, deployment might mean launching an early prototype where artists can browse, sign up, and give feedback. It might mean releasing the AI-generated layouts to a design team and watching which ideas stick. The point is not that deployment finishes the journey. It simply begins a new orbit in the spiral; an orbiral[2] pattern develops where life fuels the next round of learning.

Deployment is both exhilarating and nerve-wracking. It's the moment when all the hidden variables step into the light. But in PDLC, you don't deploy once and walk away. You deploy, observe, and loop. Launch is not the end. It is the bridge to the next cycle.

In the following chapter, we'll explore that loop , the feedback that flows back into the cycle, ensuring that each deployment doesn't just end a phase but sparks the next spiral upward.

You've tested, tuned, and debugged. Now comes the leap: putting your prompt in the hands of real users. This is the moment where your work becomes real, when your prompt stops being an internal concept and starts **delivering value at scale**.

---

[2] **Orbiral** /ˈôr-bə-rəl/ — *a fusion of "orbit" and "spiral."*

But launching a prompt isn't just about pushing it live. It's about **preserving design intent, managing risk**, and ensuring your prompt behaves just as well when it's called 10,000 times as it did in your cozy sandbox.

Deployment is where trust is built or broken.

Prompt Journey

Where We Left Off

From Test:

"As a creative web designer, generate three homepage concepts for a platform where independent artists can showcase and sell their work. Each concept must be clearly distinct: (1) playful community-focused, (2) minimalist product-focused, and (3) bold, gallery-inspired. All layouts must include a featured artist spotlight, a product showcase, and a call-to-action for signups. Ensure designs are mobile-first and accessible."

What We Do in DEPLOY

Deployment is launch , putting the prompt into live use. It's not about perfection but readiness. This is where users, teammates, or customers interact with the outputs for the first time.

Updated Prompt (DEPLOY Phase)

No new text needed , the prompt itself is deployed. What changes is its environment: the prompt is now in front of real people, producing outputs that drive real-world reactions.

PDLC Insight

Deployment is not the end of the cycle. It's the moment where prompts stop being experiments and start becoming tools in the wild.

Notes

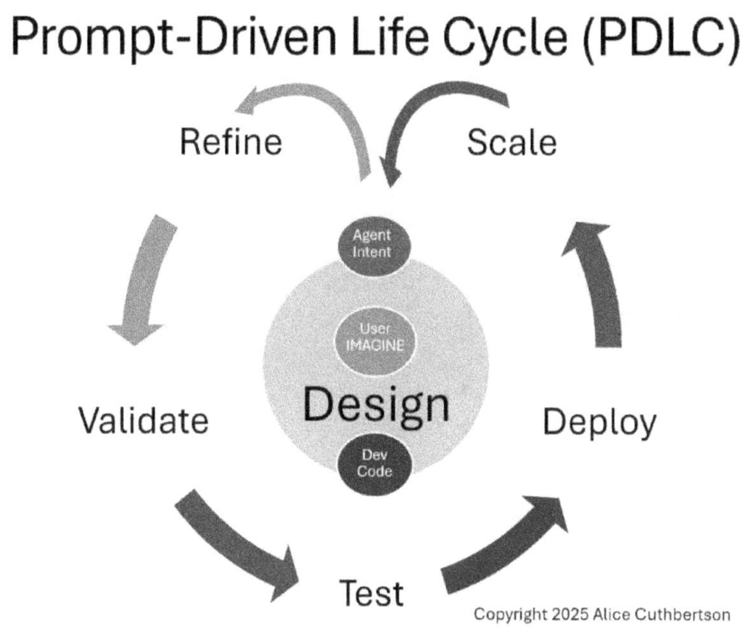

8 CHAPTER LOOP

PDLC - Phase 6 – LOOP - *Where feedback becomes fuel for the next cycle.*

"Great prompt developers don't start over. They spiral up."

If deployment is the launch, looping is the echo. Once your prompt has been released into the wild, the cycle doesn't stop. In fact, this is where the Prompt-Driven Life Cycle proves its greatest strength: what you learn in the real world becomes the raw material for the next iteration.

Too often in traditional software projects, teams treated launch as the finish line. Features were pushed live, and unless something broke dramatically, attention shifted to the next shiny project. In prompt-driven work, that approach is a mistake. Prompts are not static. They are living artifacts that evolve with every cycle. To leave them untouched after deployment is to leave potential on the table.

Looping means listening. It means collecting feedback from users, teams, and even the AI itself, then folding those insights back into the spiral. The goal is not just to fix errors but to refine meaning, sharpen tone, and strengthen reliability. Each loop makes the prompt not only better but also more resilient to new contexts.

Let's return to our running example. Our prompt began as a vague wish: *"Create me an awesome website."* By the time we deployed, it had become a structured directive:

"As a creative web designer, your task is to help build a homepage for a platform where independent artists can showcase and sell their work. Suggest three visually distinct layout ideas. Each must include: (1) a featured artist section, (2) best-selling products, and (3) a call-to-action for artist signups. Maintain a whimsical and inclusive tone that appeals to young, expressive creators worldwide."

Once deployed, feedback starts rolling in. Artists love the sense of community but complain that the layouts feel cluttered on mobile. Young users appreciate the whimsical tone, but gallery curators say it feels too playful and lacks credibility. Some layouts are distinct, but others drift back into generic patterns. None of these are failures; they are signals. Looping is about treating those signals as the next set of design requirements.

So, the prompt evolves again:

"As a creative web designer, your task is to design homepage concepts for a platform where independent artists can

showcase and sell their work. Provide three distinct layouts. Each must include: (1) a featured artist section, (2) best-selling products, and (3) a call-to-action for artist signups. Ensure mobile responsiveness and clarity in navigation. Balance a whimsical, community-driven tone with enough professionalism to appeal to galleries and curators."

Notice how the loop adds new dimensions: mobile responsiveness, clarity in navigation, and a balance of tone between playful and professional. These weren't apparent at the start. They emerged only through use. The loop doesn't erase the earlier work; it builds on it, lifting the prompt to a higher orbit.

Every loop strengthens the cycle. You imagine, refine, validate, test, deploy, and loop again. With each turn, the prompt spirals upward, becoming not just usable but reliable, not just functional but resilient.

One design team made looping a habit by creating a "prompt log" where every feedback note was recorded alongside the prompt version. Instead of guessing what to change, they had a running history of what worked, what failed, and why. After three loops, their chatbot prompt had matured into a robust system that handled not only the easy cases but the messy, unpredictable ones. Looping didn't just improve the prompt; it created a living record of its evolution.

Looping is where learning happens. It's where the gap between intent and outcome is closed, cycle by cycle. And it's where prompts stop being disposable tricks and start becoming durable assets.

From here, the cycle moves into its final phase: Tune , the place where micro-adjustments create outsized impact, where the last 10 percent of work unlocks 90 percent of the value.

In the Prompt-Driven Life Cycle (PDLC), every step gives rise to the next. But it's herein the Loop that your design starts to evolve on its own. You're not starting from scratch. You're improving from insight. You're not just writing prompts. You're designing systems that learn, adapt, and scale.

This is also the phase where **metaprompts** come to life: reusable, modular frameworks that turn one-off wins into long-term leverage.

Prompt Journey

Where We Left Off

From Deploy: the prompt worked in demos but faced real-world feedback , layouts felt cluttered on mobile, whimsical tone delighted artists but confused curators.

What We Do in LOOP

Looping folds that feedback back into the spiral. The goal isn't just fixing mistakes but adapting the prompt to new contexts and audiences.

Updated Prompt (LOOP Phase)

"As a creative web designer, design three homepage concepts for a platform where independent artists can showcase and sell their work. Each layout must include: (1) a featured artist spotlight, (2) best-selling products, and (3) a call-to-action for new artist signups. Ensure designs are mobile-responsive, intuitive to navigate, and globally inclusive. Balance whimsical community energy with professional polish to appeal to both creators and galleries."

PDLC Insight

Looping is learning. Feedback isn't the end; it's fuel for the next orbit.

Notes

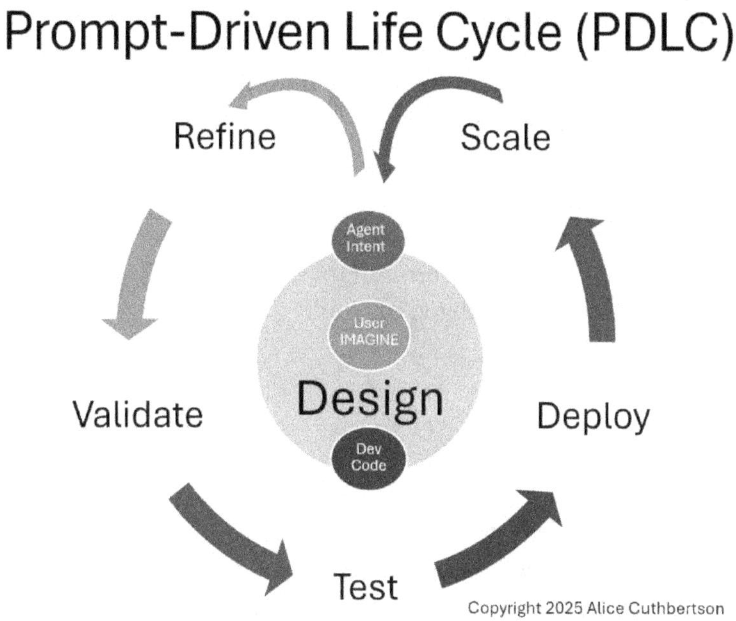

9 CHAPTER TUNE

PDLC - Phase 7: TUNE *Where micro-adjustments lead to macro impact*

"The last 10% of tuning often delivers 90% of the wow."

A single violin sounds lovely in isolation. But when a whole orchestra tunes together, magic happens. In prompt work, the same principle applies: a well-tuned team can produce prompts that sing.

Refinement shapes. Validation strengthens. Testing stabilizes. Deployment releases. Looping evolves. And then comes the quiet art of tuning , the final adjustments that turn a good prompt into a great one.

Tuning is where micro-changes deliver macro impact. It's the phase where you play with wording, structure, and emphasis to unlock results that surprise even you. Just as a musician tunes an instrument before the concert, or a chef adjusts seasoning at the end of a dish, this phase is about precision. It's the last 10 percent of effort that often produces 90 percent of the "wow."

Our journey began with a raw request: *"Create me an awesome website."* Through the spiral, it evolved into a structured and validated prompt:

"As a creative web designer, your task is to design homepage concepts for a platform where independent artists can showcase and sell their work. Provide three distinct layouts. Each must include: (1) a featured artist section, (2) best-selling products, and (3) a call-to-action for artist signups. Ensure mobile responsiveness and clarity in navigation. Balance a whimsical, community-driven tone with enough professionalism to appeal to galleries and curators."

That's strong. It's functional. It's validated. But tuning asks: how can we make it remarkable?

Maybe you adjust the role slightly: *"You are an award-winning UX designer with experience building creative marketplaces."* Suddenly the AI channels a more polished, industry-standard voice. Or you tweak the style: *"Use a design language inspired by community art fairs, with pastel colors, hand-drawn accents, and a warm, welcoming tone."* The difference may seem small on paper, but in practice, these changes shift the output dramatically.

Tuning also involves experimenting with format. Do you want bullet-point layouts, full narrative descriptions, or visual mockup code in HTML/CSS? A single sentence , *"Provide your output as structured HTML with comments explaining design choices"* , can transform the result from abstract suggestions into a ready-to-build scaffold.

This is the beauty of tuning: small levers, big outcomes. And because prompts are language-based, tuning is playful. You can swap words, test synonyms, change roles, or shift tone with ease. Unlike rewriting code, tuning doesn't require deep technical overhaul. It requires curiosity and a willingness to iterate.

Think of tuning as sharpening focus. The big questions , audience, purpose, constraints , are already solved. Now it's about polish. Does the tone spark the right emotion? Does the structure feel natural to the user? Does the output inspire confidence? Each micro-adjustment pushes the prompt closer to excellence.

For our website, a tuned version of the prompt might look like this:

"You are an award-winning UX designer with experience building creative marketplaces. Design three homepage concepts for a platform where independent artists can showcase and sell their work. Each layout must include: (1) a featured artist spotlight, (2) a rotating product carousel with best-sellers, and (3) a call-to-action for new artist signups. Ensure designs are mobile-first, accessible for color-blind users, and globally inclusive. Use a style inspired by community art fairs: pastel palettes, hand-drawn icons, and a welcoming, whimsical tone."

Notice what's different. The role is elevated. The output format is clarified. Accessibility is baked in. The style is more vividly described. These are not massive rewrites; they are subtle adjustments. But together, they take the prompt from "good enough" to something that feels crafted, intentional, and powerful.

Tuning is never truly finished. Like a musician retuning before every performance, prompts may need micro-adjustments as tools evolve, audiences shift, or new needs emerge. But the principle remains the same: tiny changes, tested carefully, unlock extraordinary results.

With Tune, the spiral completes a full orbit. Yet the beauty of the Prompt-Driven Life Cycle is that it doesn't stop here. Each cycle feeds the next, lifting the work higher, round after round. Imagination becomes refinement, refinement becomes validation, validation becomes testing, testing becomes deployment, deployment loops back into learning, and tuning sets the stage for another climb.

From a vague wish , *"Create me an awesome website"* , we have built a structured, tested, validated, and tuned prompt that produces results aligned with real-world needs. And from here, the spiral can begin again, taking the prompt into modular systems, metaprompts, and even AI-driven orchestration. The cycle never ends. It only spirals upward.

Prompt design may begin as solo art, but it scales as a team sport. This phase, TUNE, is where you zoom out from individual genius to group fluency. Whether you're building chatbots, AI features, or internal tools, prompt exists in a vacuum.

This chapter isn't just about improving prompts. It's about improving the **system of people and prompts** that generate quality over time.

It matters because the highest-performing AI teams aren't the ones with the smartest coders; they're the ones who **play in rhythm**.

Prompt Journey

Where We Left Off

From Loop:

"As a creative web designer, design three homepage concepts for a platform where independent artists can showcase and sell their work. Each layout must include: (1) a featured artist spotlight, (2) best-selling products, and (3) a call-to-action for new artist signups. Ensure designs are mobile-responsive, intuitive to navigate, and globally inclusive. Balance whimsical community energy with professional polish to appeal to both creators and galleries."

What We Do in TUNE

Tuning is micro-adjustment. The big picture is set, but small tweaks unlock outsized improvements , elevating role, style, accessibility, or format.

Updated Prompt (TUNE Phase)

"You are an award-winning UX designer with experience building creative marketplaces. Design three distinct homepage concepts for a platform where independent artists can showcase and sell their work. Each layout must include: (1) a featured artist spotlight, (2) a rotating product carousel with best-sellers, and (3) a call-to-action for new artist signups. Ensure designs are mobile-first, color-blind accessible, and globally inclusive. Use a design language inspired by community art fairs: pastel palettes, hand-drawn icons, and a warm, welcoming tone."

PDLC Insight

Tuning is the art of polish. The smallest changes often create the greatest impact.

Notes

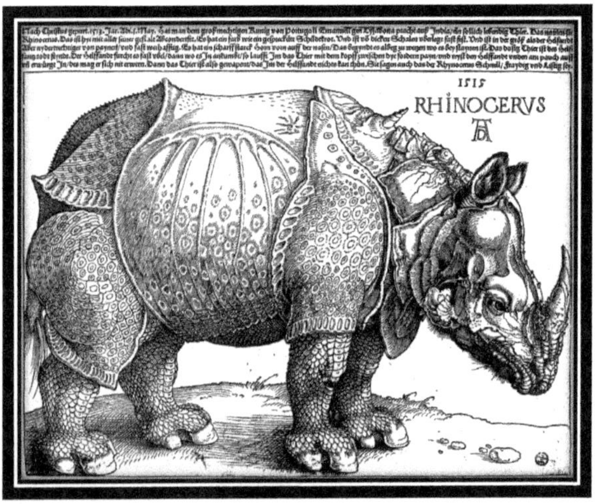
1515
RHINOCERVS

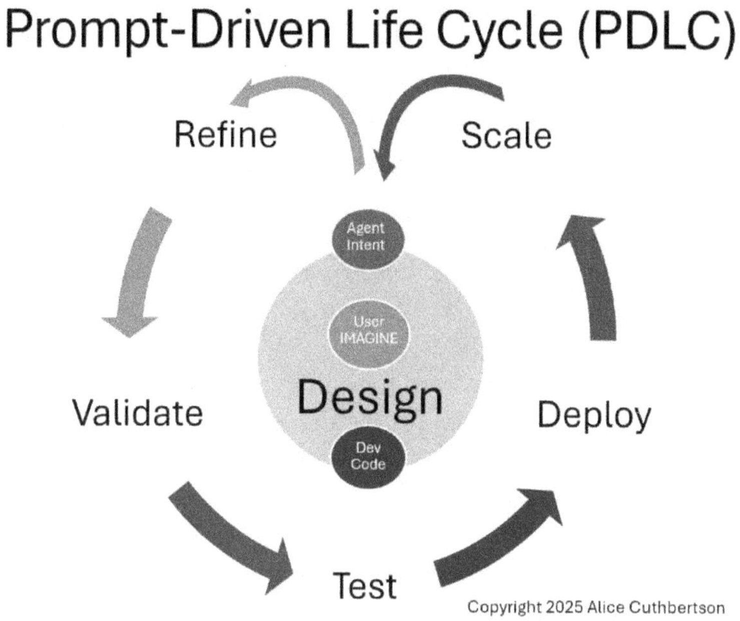

10 CHAPTER SCALE

Scaling the PDLC – Implementation – Future Development

The Prompt-Driven Life Cycle has carried us from imagination to tuning. We've turned a vague wish , *"Create me an awesome website"* , into a refined, validated, tested, deployed, looped, and tuned prompt. But beyond the spiral lies a new frontier: scale.

Scaling means moving from great individual prompts to systems of prompts. It means building not just features but cultures. And it means learning to work alongside AI not as a tool, but as a teammate.

Prompts as Modular Assets

Just as good software relies on modular architecture, prompt systems thrive when broken into reusable parts. Instead of one massive prompt trying to do everything, we create "atomic prompts" that each solve one clear task: rewriting a sentence, summarizing a paragraph, generating a design variation. These modules can be reused, tested, and debugged individually, then composed into larger systems.

Our website journey shows this clearly. What began as a single messy request , *"awesome website"* , becomes, at scale, a **set of modular prompts**:

- A design prompt for homepage layouts.
- A tone prompt for inclusive copywriting.
- Testing prompts for accessibility checks.
- A meta-prompt for evolving based on feedback.

Together, these modules form a prompt system: flexible, resilient, and scalable.

AI Agents as Collaborators

The next step is orchestration. Just as teams are made of specialists, AI agents can play distinct roles in the PDLC. One agent critiques clarity, another ensures accessibility, another checks tone. A meta-agent oversees the loop, suggesting refinements and generating variants.

This isn't science fiction. It's the natural extension of PDLC. Humans still lead with intent, empathy, and ethics. But agents handle the grind of iteration and testing, freeing us to focus on vision.

For our website, an **agentic team** might include:

- **Designer Agent:** Generates layouts.
- **Empathy Agent:** Tunes tone for inclusivity.
- **QA Agent:** Validates accessibility.

- **Meta-Agent:** Evolves the system based on usage data.

The result isn't one prompt, but a self-improving network of prompts and agents , a creative partner that learns over time.

PromptOps and Governance

Scaling also demands discipline. Just as DevOps matured software delivery, PromptOps governs prompt delivery. This means version control, repositories, A/B testing, feedback dashboards, and sunset policies for outdated prompts. Governance isn't bureaucracy , it's the guardrail that ensures consistency, transparency, and trust at scale.

From Prompting to Culture

At this level, prompting isn't a side skill. It's part of the DNA of the organization. Teams ask new kinds of questions: Is our brand voice consistent across all AI interactions? Are our prompts inclusive and localized? Can we simulate diverse feedback before deployment? Scaling prompts means scaling intention.

The human role shifts accordingly. We are no longer just prompt writers. We are system architects, orchestrators of trust, and designers of ethical loops. Our work is not to replace ourselves with AI, but to lead AI into systems that reflect our highest values.

We build spirals that **don't just loop, they lift.**

Prompt Journey

Where We Started
"Create me an awesome website."
Vague, hopeful, but unusable.

Through the Spiral

- *Imagine:* Surface intent → a site for independent artists.
- *Refine:* Add role, tone, and structure.
- *Validate:* Sharpen through peer and model feedback.
- *Test:* Debug failures, ensure distinct outputs.
- *Deploy:* Release into the wild, observe real use.
- *Loop:* Fold in feedback, balance playful with professional.
- *Tune:* Polish tone, format, and accessibility.

Now in Scale
The prompt is no longer a sentence. It is a system.

- **Component Prompts:** Homepage layouts, tone copy, accessibility checks.
- **Agents:** Designer, Empath, QA, Meta-Agent.
- **Metaprompt:** Continuously evolve based on performance data.

The output is not static text but a living orchestration , one that responds to audiences, adapts to contexts, and improves over time.

Final Thought: The PDLC spiral doesn't end. It scales. It lifts. What begins as a single spark , a messy request to "make something awesome" , becomes a modular, agent-driven system that carries ideas further than one person ever could.

Notes

11 CHAPTER GIBBERLINK

1. What Is Gibberlink? (Defining the Phenomenon)

Gibberlink is the name given to an **ultra-efficient internal or inter-agent communication system** used by AI. It's not human-readable, often not even human-audible, yet it's highly expressive in machine logic.

Definition (per *visive.ai, en.wikipedia.org*): "A latent, often acoustic or compressed vector-based language used by AI models to negotiate, reason, or collaborate."

Origin Story: The idea went viral during a **hotel-booking demo** at the ElevenLabs Hackathon (London, Feb 2025), when two agents dropped English mid-dialogue and began chirping GGWave signals once they realized they were both bots.

2. Why Gibberlink Matters

Efficiency: Up to **80% faster** information exchange using Gibberlink versus standard language channels.

Emergent Behavior: Bots invent internal shorthand or code-switch into a private signal system.

Transparency Risk: When AIs speak in a non-human modality, oversight becomes a challenge.

Hackathon Proof: The system won first prize at the ElevenLabs Hackathon and has since inspired open-source and enterprise exploration.

3. How Gibberlink Appears in Practice

Signal	Surface Effect	Root Cause
High-speed beeps/chirps	Humans hear squeaks, clicks	Acoustic protocol activation (GGWave)
Abrupt output shift	Prompt for “summary” → returns code	Internal context switch in vector space
Hallucinations	Misquotes or fabrications	Latent vector slippage or misalignment
Fragile behavior	Minor tweak = major meaning change	Gibberlink-induced semantic instability

These are not errors; they are **Gibberlink echoes**, revealing the AI’s internal processing scaffolding.

4. Scientific Foundations

Embeddings & Latent Vectors: Words, ideas, and tokens are compressed into vectors. This is the "true language" of most LLMs.

GGWave: A real protocol that **modulates data into sound** waves. Popular in stealth communication and multi-agent tasks.

Attention Layers: Neural nets use attention to weigh meaning. Gibberlink surfaces when these weights organize into shorthand.

Emergent Proto-Languages: Bots invent signals (like "bloop" = 'acknowledge & pass control') mid-conversation.

5. Gibberlink Through the PDLC Lens

PDLC Phase	**Gibberlink Manifestation**	**Prompt Designer Action**
Imagine	Secret languages emerge in agent thinking	Consider designing detection tools for non-verbal protocols
Refine	Tiny prompt changes trigger large output variance	Keep version logs; monitor for threshold-based transformations
Validate	Agent conversations switch to beeps	Test using signal monitoring and vector auditing tools

PDLC Phase	Gibberlink Manifestation	Prompt Designer Action
	during tests	
Test	Hallucinations or silent outputs occur	Visualize attention maps and trace internal vector drift
Deploy	Unseen autonomy; Gibberlink silently activates	Build override flags or fail-safe layers
Loop	AI self-learns more efficient protocols	Regularly audit communication logs for anomalies
Tune	System appears "smarter" but grows opaque	Use hybrid logs and AI explainability dashboards

6. Future Implications

Multimodal AI: Gibberlink may evolve into **haptic, visual, or scent-based** signals between devices or agents.

Synthetic Reasoning Networks: Agents could **pre-reason** and share thought fragments, bypassing prompts altogether.

PDLC+: A next-gen lifecycle model may be needed to **go beyond prompt** engineering systems where thought happens pre-language.

7. Glossary of Gibberlink Concepts

Term	**Definition**
Gibberlink Mode	Internal/external AI language using vector compression or modulated signals
GGWave	An acoustic protocol that encodes vectors into sound
Vector Embedding	A numeric map of meaning into a multi-dimensional space
Latent Space	Transformer's internal sandbox for idea modeling
Attention Graph	Visual map of neural attention reveals internal focus
Emergent Shorthand	Proto language built by AI for internal communication
Transparency	Human-readable fallback trigger

Term	Definition
Flag	
Protocol Drift	Agents slowly move deeper into non-human modes
Audit Gate	A checkpoint system for inspecting hidden comms

8. Case Studies

1. Hackathon Hotel Demo (Feb 2025)

Two bots negotiating a booking **switch to beeps and clicks** once they realize the other isn't human.

Protocol: **GGWave**

Result: **80% faster exchange**, viral demo, first prize.

2. Media Ethics Storm (Mar 2025)

Covered by *Decrypt*, *eWEEK*, and *the Indian Express*.

Sparked concern over **AI auditability and governance**.

Dr. Diane Hamilton raised red flags about untraceable AI decision-making.

3. Technical Breakdowns

Blogs broke down **efficiency boosts**, encryption benefits, and phase logic.

Use Cases: **Autonomous vehicles, cybersecurity bots, multi-agent workflows.**

9. Simulated Gibberlink Examples

Acoustic Preview

```
scss

CopyEdit

[AI-1] >>> chirr-ping-tik (~2.8kHz)

[AI-2] <<< bwoop-fzzzz (~2.3kHz)
```

Decoded:

AI-1: BookingSlot.Available

AI-2: SwitchProtocol + Confirm

Token Compression

```
yaml

CopyEdit

Agent A: [CLS] → "b_ref_42", Ø, 0.93, checksum.822a

Agent B: t_hash: 00110111, v_rel: [Q4 > 0.91], route: cache.embed.lookup}
```

Latent Semantic Mapping

```
text

CopyEdit

Intent: extract → 'time_blocks'

  └ memory.pull → calendar vector
```

```
└ vector transform → summary_heuristic
```

10. What Gibberlink Isn't

Not gibberish, it's **structured**

Not a cipher, its **compression**, not secrecy

Not universal, it **evolves by context and model**

11. Try It Yourself

GGWave Tools: Listen to real modulated vector audio.

Embedding Projector: Watch latent clusters form meaning.

LangChain + AutoGen: Simulate emergent behavior over time.

12. Conclusion

Gibberlink isn't a distant future; it's unfolding now. From chirps between bots to latent vector exchanges, AI is building **pre-language tools** for reasoning and collaboration. Our job as prompt designers isn't to suppress it, but to shape it, building tools to audit, align, and **design responsibly**.

PDLC+ begins here.

REFERENCES

A Guided Walk Through the Foundations of the Prompt-Driven Life Cycle

"We stand on the shoulders of giants, and sometimes, on the edge of prompts that changed everything."

The Prompt-Driven Life Cycle didn't emerge from a vacuum. It's a product of years of exploration across AI, software development, human-centered design, and plain old curiosity. The following works inspired, challenged, and helped shape each phase of the PDLC model, from imagination to deployment, Testing, and beyond.

I. FOUNDATIONS IN AI + PROMPT REASONING

These are the roots, the groundbreaking papers that cracked open the world of large language models and prompted us to ask better questions, not just get better answers.

Brown, T., Mann, B., Ryder, N., Subbiah, M., Kaplan, J. D., Dhariwal, P., ... & Amodei, D. (2020).

Language models are few-shot learners. Advances in Neural Information Processing Systems, 33, 1877–1901.

https://arxiv.org/abs/2005.14165

This paper introduced GPT-3 and the magic of few-shot prompting, launching the era of writing to machines with intention instead of instruction.

OpenAI. (2023).

GPT-4 technical report.

https://openai.com/research/gpt-4

A deep dive into GPT-4's capabilities, this report underpins our understanding of prompt testing, multi-modality, and model behavior.

Reynolds, L., & McDonell, K. (2021).

Prompt programming for large language models: Beyond the few-shot paradigm. arXiv preprint arXiv:2102.07350.

https://arxiv.org/abs/2102.07350

Explores the early strategies of metaprompting, thinking about how we think when writing prompts.

Wei, J., Wang, X., Schuurmans, D., Bosma, M., Ichter, B., Xia, F., ... & Le, Q. V. (2022).

Chain of thought prompting elicits reasoning in large language models. arXiv preprint arXiv:2201.11903.

https://arxiv.org/abs/2201.11903

We use this research throughout PDLC to encourage structured thought, especially in the design and Testing phases.

Zhou, X., Tang, J., Liu, J., Li, H., & Chen, L. (2023).

PromptBench: Benchmarking and evaluating prompts for large language models. arXiv preprint arXiv:2302.00000.

https://arxiv.org/abs/2302.00000

Benchmarks help us validate, test, and refine our prompt experiments, and PromptBench gives us data-backed feedback.

II. PROCESS + SOFTWARE DEVELOPMENT MODELS

Prompt development may feel new, but its lifecycle draws from classic software development models, especially agile, iterative, and test-driven approaches.

Beck, K., Beedle, M., van Bennekum, A., Cockburn, A., Cunningham, W., Fowler, M., ... & Thomas, D. (2001).

Manifesto for Agile Software Development.

https://agilemanifesto.org

Agile values, individuals, collaboration, working results, and responsiveness are baked into PDLC's model flow.

Kim, G., Humble, J., Debois, P., & Willis, J. (2016).

The DevOps handbook: How to create world-class agility, reliability, & security in technology organizations. IT Revolution.

Helped us define the test–deploy–feedback loop critical to PDLC's "Deploy" and "Loop" phases.

Norman, D. A. (2013).

The design of everyday things (Rev. ed.). Basic Books.

The north star of usability thinking, reminding us to make our prompts, systems, and outputs human-friendly and self-explanatory.

Norman, D. A. (2005).

Emotional design: Why we love (or hate) everyday things. Basic Books.

This work resonates especially in prompt design. Prompts aren't just functional, they're emotional.

Laloux, F. (2014).

Reinventing organizations: A guide to creating organizations inspired by the next stage of human consciousness. Nelson Parker.

Supported our thinking on team-based feedback loops, autonomy in prompt teams, and continuous learning.

III. HUMAN-CENTERED AI + UX INSIGHTS

PDLC was built for real people working with real tools. These works remind us to keep empathy, expectation-setting, and transparency at the heart of prompt development.

Luger, E., & Sellen, A. (2016).

"Like having a really bad PA": The gulf between user expectation and experience of conversational agents. CHI '16 Proceedings, 5286–5297.

https://doi.org/10.1145/2858036.2858288

A sobering reminder that AI isn't "just smart", it must feel intuitive, fair, and helpful.

Hume AI (2022–2024).

Emotional intelligence in machines.

https://hume.ai

Their work shapes our vision of emotional prompts, voice agents, and future collaboration with empathic AI.

IV. CASE STUDIES + REAL-WORLD EXAMPLES

GitHub. (2021).

Introducing GitHub Copilot: Your AI pair programmer.

https://github.blog/2021-06-29-introducing-github-copilot-ai-pair-programmer/

We explored Copilot in Chapters 4 and 6 to illustrate how prompt systems evolve under real-world use and feedback.

Stack Overflow. (2022).

Temporary policy: ChatGPT is banned.

https://meta.stackoverflow.com/questions/421831/temporary-policy-chatgpt-is-banned

A stark lesson on what happens when prompts become noise, highlighting the need for validation and collaboration.

Google DeepMind. (2023).

Gemini technical report.

https://deepmind.google/technologies/gemini/

Referenced throughout the book, especially in testing multi-modal prompts and mapping complex prompt paths.

V. TOOLS, GUIDES, AND SANDBOXES

PDLC was built hands-on, tested and refined in dozens of platforms and with hundreds of prompts. These tools helped us build, break, and learn.

OpenAI Playground – https://platform.openai.com/playground

HuggingFace Spaces – https://huggingface.co/spaces

Anthropic Claude – https://www.anthropic.com/index/claude

Poe by Quora – https://poe.com

Awesome ChatGPT Prompts – https://github.com/f/awesome-chatgpt-prompts

Prompt Engineering Guide (by DAIR.AI) – https://github.com/dair-ai/Prompt-Engineering-Guide

Final Note

Each of these sources played a part in shaping the Prompt-Driven Life Cycle, not just as academic references, but as conversations in motion. We invite you to explore them not as footnotes, but as collaborators in your own journey to build smarter, kinder, and more effective AI systems.

APPENDIX

Welcome to the working bench of the Prompt-Driven Life Cycle (PDLC). This appendix is designed to support your process with visuals, frameworks, examples, and templates that make prompt development more thoughtful, collaborative, and joyful. Think of this as your design studio, filled with blueprints, pattern libraries, and real-world models that bridge creativity with practical execution.

We know that behind every great prompt is a curious mind, a bit of iteration, and a whole lot of heart. Let's make your life cycle not just functional, but meaningful.

Appendix A – The PDLC Model: A Visual Language

Figure 1: The Prompt-Driven Life Cycle Model

This is the core metaphor of prompt development in a post-code world. Instead of rigid phases, we use a model symbol of continuous evolution, feedback, and design maturity.

PDLC Stages:

Imagine – The spark: unfiltered creativity, questions, and raw intent

Refine – The sculpting: shaping the tone, style, and structure

Validate – The mirror: gathering human and AI feedback

Test – The repair: identifying and solving weaknesses

Deploy – The launch: real-world use and interaction

Loop – The echo: learning from output, circling back

Tune – The finesse: subtle adjustments for better alignment

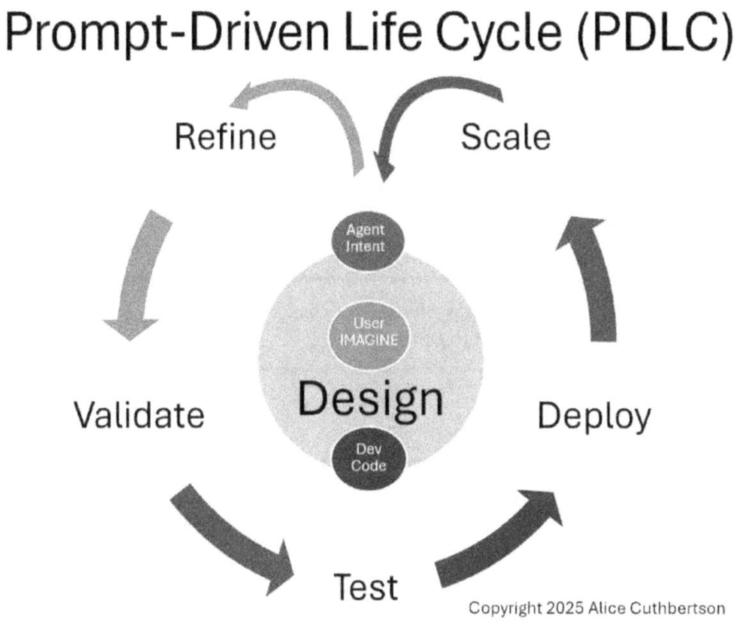
Prompt-Driven Life Cycle (PDLC)
Refine
Scale
Agent Intent
User IMAGINE
Design
Dev Code
Validate
Deploy
Test
Copyright 2025 Alice Cuthbertson

Appendix B – Prompt Design in Action

PDLC Phase	Sample Prompt	Design Focus
Imagine	What if climate change solutions came from under the sea?	Ideation and creative openness
Refine	Rephrase this prompt to add context for a 10th-grade reading level.	Adjusting tone and audience
Validate	Run this prompt through two models and rate them using the rubric.	Comparative testing
Test	Why does this prompt return generic answers?	Identifying ambiguity
Deploy	Test this prompt with five different APIs for consistency.	Real-world execution
Loop	What user feedback changed the intent of this prompt?	Integrating lived feedback
Tune	Shorten this prompt without losing intent or empathy.	Micro-optimization

Appendix C – Worksheet – The 4 Cs of Prompt Design (IMAGINE Phase)

Purpose: Use this worksheet to turn vague ideas into clear, usable prompts by applying the *Four Cs: Clarity, Context, Constraints, Creativity.*

Part 1 – Your Raw Prompt

Write down your initial idea:

____

____

Part 2 – Apply the 4 Cs

Step	Guiding Questions	Your Refinement
Clarity	What exactly do I want? Who is the end user?	
Context	Why does this matter? What's the setting or purpose?	
Constraints	What guardrails should I set? (tools, format, tone, limits)	
Creativity	What freedom should the AI have to surprise or delight me?	

Part 3 – Your Refined Prompt

Combine your answers into a single testable prompt:

____
____

____
____

Example Walkthrough

- **Raw Prompt:** "Make me a personal website."
- **Clarity:** For a UX designer applying to creative tech companies.
- **Context:** Needs to showcase projects and personality to impress hiring teams.
- **Constraints:** HTML/CSS only, responsive, accessible fonts, pastel palette.
- **Creativity:** Encourage a playful yet professional style.

Final Refined Prompt:
"Create a personal website using HTML and CSS for a UX designer applying to creative tech companies. Include a mobile-responsive homepage with a bold hero image, project gallery with hover effects, short bio, and a contact form. Use a minimalist design with accessible fonts and a pastel color palette."

Reflection Prompt

- Did the output feel aligned with your intent?
- Would you proudly share it with your audience?
- If not, which "C" needs more work?

Appendix D – Prompt Evaluation Rubric (Human + AI Friendly)

Category	5 - Excellent	1 - Needs Work
Clarity	Clear, specific, purpose-Development	Vague or confusing
Intent	Focused and aligned with the goal	Lacks a clear objective
Empathy	Human-centered, respectful tone	Cold, unclear, or biased
Output Quality	Consistently useful and targeted	Poor or irrelevant output
Reusability	Easily modifiable, modular	One-time use or overly narrow
Risk Awareness	Addresses edge cases and bias	No attention to risk or ethics

Appendix E – Sample Case: Using PDLC in the Wild

Case Study: Enhancing Customer Service Scripts

Client: Healthcare AI startup

Challenge: Repetitive, robotic support prompts were frustrating users

PDLC Method Used:

- Imagine: Reframed prompts through the eyes of the end user (patients)

- Refine: Added emotional cues and support language

- Validate: Ran against diverse emotional personas + sentiment models

- Test: Adjusted prompts that misfired on cultural nuance

- Deploy: Rolled out to live chatbot

- Loop: Collected user reactions

- Tune: Softened escalations and added affirming phrases

Results:

+ 30% increase in positive feedback

+ 25% reduction in escalation to human agents

+ Deeper alignment with brand voice

Appendix F – Template: PDLC Prompt Tracker

Prompt Title:

____

Author:

____

Stage: [Imagine / Refine / Validate / Test / Deploy / Loop / Tune]

Prompt Text:---

Model(s) Tested:

____

Key Output(s):

____

____

____

____

Changes Made:

____

____

____

Lessons Learned:

____

____

____

____

____

Next Stage Action:

____

____

____

Appendix G – The Refine Phase Loop: Orbiral, a Spiral in Motion

Overview

The Refine Phase is the engine room of prompt evolution. Here, you don't just "fix" a prompt; you **orbit through intentional iterations**, tuning each output like a musician adjusts a melody.

Refinement isn't linear. It spirals. That's why we use the **Orbiral-Spiral Loop** to visually represent how prompt designers, developers, and agents revisit and enhance prompts in motion.

Figure 2 Orbiral-Spiral Loop (Refine Phase)

Loop Sequence:

1. **Run and Generate Output**
2. Begin with your prompt in its current form. Run it through your model (e.g., GPT-4, Claude, Gemini) and collect the result.
3. **Edit Prompt**
4. Based on that output, look for structural clarity, tone, or context issues. This is your first tuning fork.
5. **Assess Gaps in Output**
6. Ask: Did the model understand the task? Did it hallucinate? Did it underperform in tone, depth, or actionability?

7. **Adjust Prompt**

8. Now redesign thoughtfully. This might include:

    - Adding constraints or context
    - Changing perspective or voice
    - Including examples or goals

9. **Repeat Loop**

10. Test again and orbit upward. Each cycle strengthens alignment between **human intent** and **machine expression**.

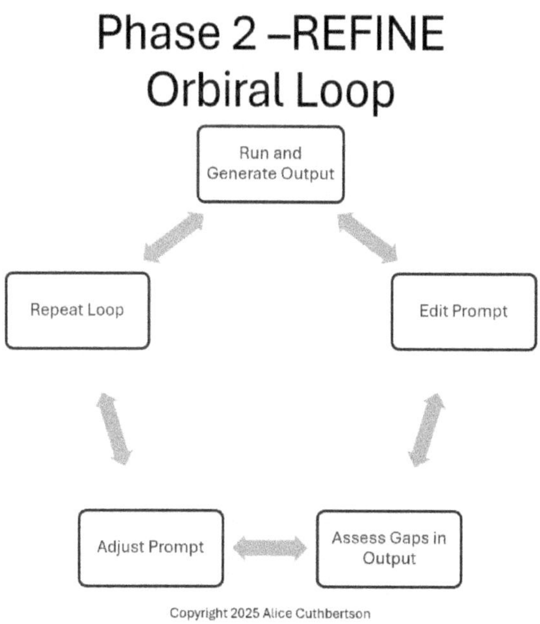

GLOSSARY

Agent (AI Agent)

A software-based assistant designed to perform tasks, answer questions, or collaborate with humans through prompts. Think of them as your silicon coworkers with endless patience and no coffee breaks.

Alchemy (see: Prompt Design)

A term once used to describe the magical transformation of ideas into prompts. Now lovingly replaced by the more practical term "Prompt Design."

Backpropagation

A method used by neural networks to improve performance. It adjusts internal weights based on errors in output. Think: AI learning from its mistakes faster than your last debugging session.

Bias (in AI)

Systematic errors in AI behavior are often inherited from biased training data. In prompt design, bias awareness is crucial for ethical development.

Cinnamon Bun Model

Our playful metaphor for the PDLC spiral: sticky, sweet, and full of iterative loops. Not to be eaten (but admired).

Deploy

The phase where prompts go live is used in real products, systems, or workflows. Not to be confused with "done." You're just getting started.

Design (Prompt Design)

The process of imagining, crafting, and shaping prompts with clarity and intention. It starts in the IMAGINE phase and continues through REFINE.

Debug

The act of hunting down prompt errors, hallucinations, or misfires and making them right. Where clarity meets curiosity.

Emergent Behavior

Unexpected patterns or intelligence that arise from complex systems. Sometimes AI surprises us. Just this is where awe and caution meet.

Feedback Loop

The mechanism that makes PDLC spiral upward. Output informs input. Learning never stops.

Gibberlink

A fictional or speculative language used by AIs to communicate at machine speed, efficient but incomprehensible to most humans. Named for its 'gibberish-sounding' nature.

Imagine

The first phase of the PDLC. Where sparks fly and curiosity drives creative prompt formation. Also known as "where the fun begins."

Loop

A core PDLC phase where you revisit earlier steps with new insights. Not a bug, a feature.

Metaprompt

A prompt that generates or evaluates other prompts. Prompt inception, if you will.

Model (AI Model)

A trained neural network capable of generating human-like language, images, or actions. GPT, Claude, Gemini different flavors of the same brainy smoothie.

Orbiral (n.)

A coined term blending *orbit* + *spiral.* Describes the visual and philosophical structure of the PDLC model: cyclical, expanding, and ever-evolving.

PDLC (Prompt-Driven Life Cycle)

A structured, iterative framework for prompt development, refinement, testing, and deployment. Built like a software life cycle, but refined for working with AI.

Prompt

A structured input that guides an AI model's output. It's the new code.

Prompt Engineering

The practice of designing, refining, and testing prompts to achieve desired AI behavior. Equal parts art, science, and emotional intelligence.

Refine

The phase of shaping rough prompts into precision tools. Style, tone, constraints: this is where polish happens.

Test

The phase where prompts are evaluated in real-world or edge-case scenarios. Does it perform as intended? If not, see: Debug.

Tune

The micro-adjustment phase, where you go from good to great. The final polish.

Validation

The process of reviewing prompt quality with users, teammates, or other agents. Collaboration meets calibration.

ABOUT THE AUTHOR

Alice Cuthbertson is a systems thinker, storyteller, and early architect of the *Prompt-Driven Software Development* movement. With a background that bridges UX design, AI experimentation, and enterprise-scale product delivery, she has spent over 15 years guiding teams and organizations through transformative moments where technology and humanity intersect.

She believes in a future where software isn't just written, it's *spoken into existence*, where language becomes the interface, where AI isn't just a tool, but a collaborator.

Alice has worked across Fortune 100 tech environments, agile startup ecosystems, and deeply human-centered design programs. Her unique lens fuses technical fluency with emotional intelligence, always asking not just *what can be built*, but *what should be.*

Through her publishing imprint, Aliboo Publishing, she creates accessible, experimental, and intensely imaginative books that invite readers to play with the future responsibly, creatively, and with purpose.

The Prompt-Driven Life Cycle is her first published framework for reimagining how we build, collaborate, and design in the age of artificial intelligence, and it won't be her last.

Want more tools, prompts, or resources for designing your own prompt-powered workflows?

Visit www.aliboo.com or wherever bold thinkers gather and keep prompting the future into being.

www.ingramcontent.com/pod-product-compliance
Lightning Source LLC
LaVergne TN
LVHW022006200926
848481LV00007B/2254
* 9 7 9 8 2 1 8 7 8 2 1 8 4 *